Wakefield Press

Waldo's Game

Although he worries about the placement of commas, **Peter Bakowski** has been writing poetry for 41 years. He, his partner Helen, and Buzz the super poodle, actively seek out places in which to write, sew and bark, letting each new or favoured locale enter their daily lives, ways of viewing themselves, the world and creativity.

In 2015 Éditions Bruno Doucey of Paris, published a bilingual selection of Peter's poetry, titled *Le cœur à trios heures du matin*. In Australia in 2024 Hunter Publishers will publish his next solo poetry collection, *Necessary Wonder.*

A haunted figure, yet 'sunny' for all that, **Ken Bolton**, stunted, stumbling, unkempt, lives in Adelaide where for a long time he ran the Experimental Art Foundation's Dark Horsey bookshop and, with zero panache, the Lee Marvin readings. Recent collections include *Starting at Basheer's* (Vagabond) and 2022's *Fantastic Day* (from Puncher & Wattmann). Shearsman (UK) issued his *Selected Poems* in 2013, replacing a Penguin *Selected.* His romance on Life at Sea—*A Pirate Life*—was published by Cordite this year.

The complete interlinked *Elsewhere Variations* series—*The Elsewhere Variations*, *Nearly Lunch*, *Waldo's Game* and *Luck Street*—is now available from Wakefield Press.

Waldo's Game

Peter Bakowski and Ken Bolton

Wakefield
Press

Wakefield Press
16 Rose Street
Mile End
South Australia 5031
www.wakefieldpress.com.au

First published 2023

Front cover photo 'Night, Turin, Italy' by Eli Toscano
Back cover photo 'Market area, Hirakata, Japan' photo by John Levy
Edited by Polly Grant Butler, Wakefield Press
Typeset by Jesse Pollard, Wakefield Press
Original design by Michael Deves, Wakefield Press

Printed in Australia by Pegasus Media & Logistics

ISBN 978 1 92304 205 6

NATIONAL
LIBRARY
OF AUSTRALIA

A catalogue record for this
book is available from the
National Library of Australia

CORIOLE
McLAREN VALE

Wakefield Press thanks
Coriole Vineyards for
continued support

Contents

Acknowledgements

Some of these poems, or earlier versions of them, have appeared in the following magazines and journals, either in print form or online: *Hanging Loose,* (USA); *Island*; *Ostragehege* (Germany).

SIXPACK ONE

Claude Hartigan visited by journalist Roderick Bix

Since the liver transplant Claude has mellowed.

His pronouncements, the tone in which he proclaims

"Remember, the piano is a percussion instrument"

or "The imagination has no shoreline"

now invite a response rather than worship.

Claude lights his pipe, continues our conversation—

"It was 1961, in the summer holidays,

when my father drowned in the Shoalhaven River.

I sought distance from my mother, my sister and the house.

Each morning after breakfast I walked into the bush,

walked until I was footsore, thirsty, blind with sweat,

hoping to fall down a mineshaft.

The pain of blisters, bull ant bites and sunburn I understood.

There was a salve for them, in the family medicine cabinet."

"Tall, foghorn voice, a room pacer,

that was Mr. Arnott, our art teacher at Melbourne University.

He talked about compassion—to convey via paint the *aloneness*

of each flower in a vase, each person in a supermarket aisle.

What I learnt from Arnott was to reveal.

Of course, a painting may also infer—reward the scrupulous eye."

Claude recalls his London years—favourite bus routes,
shoplifting sprees, introduction to Gilda at a dinner party…
I see him make a show of glancing at his wristwatch
and I reach for my hat and scarf, both of us pleased
with the afternoon, the firmness of his handshake.

Wendy's Day

Out the door at 6.30, 7 —
& walk to the coffee shop
across the suburbs in the cool
air. Coffee. Read the papers
check the phone—& back—amble
or walk or bus even, shopping
on the way—& arrive, home
a march stolen on the day

Moses, the cat—his long, &
tender reach,
to importune food—purring.

An old cat hardly able to eat—
comforted to be remembered, a
kindness

Then to the front room.

The carpet, a pale, cream yellow—

wisps of a russet brown

upon it, irregular almost, & few—

like white coffee slightly stirred—

that enliven it, yes—& summon, or

salute, the brown in the room,

of floor & desk. And down to work.

Done That

"Go upstairs, Stefan," says Rietveld

when you enter. Stefan whips quickly

out the back of the shop. You step forward,

grab Rietveld by the ears & hold him.

You say "Waldo, you owe me,"

& are suddenly taken back—

his wide, frightened eyes,

a watery blue, & you see your grandfather

whom you held this way—once?

twice? aged one, *less than two*—

held ears, nose, jowls,

examined him closely, an

alien, a tiny mogul. "Listen pal …"

"Listen pal," you say—those same

words—& pause. Rietveld,

the broken veins, the creased &

pouchy skin, the old eyes.

Your grandfather had laughed,

remarked on your resemblance to

"a small gangster". "Rietveld,

how long has it been?"

"A month?" says Rietveld.

"Take three more," you tell him.

"Oh," says Rietveld, overcome,

"That is very generous." Shaken,

you leave. "You owe me," you say,

over your shoulder, almost

to yourself, angry.

Roderick Bix talks about Gilda Beckt with gallerist, Simon Simek

Gilda's reputation is solid. Overtures from São Paulo.

A possible exhibition there in eighteen months.

Great care would have to be taken with the shipping.

The delicate pieces, *The Golden Virgin*, for example,

the Swiss mightn't allow a work, so recently bought, to be loaned.

Gilda is also painting.

In this still fresh decade, which she sometimes calls her last,

Gilda views the blank canvas as an invitation to risk and surrender.

Of late, the subjects of her paintings have been

rodeo riders, trapeze artists and ice skaters.

"Energy is everything," she told me

when I visited her last week—

Gilda shuffling towards the studio kettle,

finding two clean cups for tea.

Form guide

J is for Jerome.

Butterfly collector—
resident species of the British Isles only.

Living on a barge
reminds Jerome of his Dutch father,
whose rare land visits
often ended in the drunk tank,
followed by a few days of civility,
but never touch or tenderness.

Hemel Hempstead is far enough from London
for Jerome to resist folding back into old habits.
The botched kidnapping, then going to ground
in various Hackney squats for a month,
have scared Jerome into the straight life.

Always good with numbers,

studying the odds, buying and re-selling

motor cars, Scandinavian furniture, vintage pinball machines,

Jerome's part owner of three racehorses.

A few regional wins.

Building up to some tryouts in Ireland,

quietly confident.

On The Sunny Side Of The Street

as I walk to Allan & Linda's
I stop, & watch a spider
fight an enormous wasp a few
metres away. I pause—& observe.

After, I'd bid a woman my age *Nice day!*
as we drew level & passed.
It was a day for bidding.

I stopped for the spider, & the
giant thing it fought,
a wasp? but big—'*two inches*'—
the spider backed & circled, kept its face
to the foe—which looked bigger than it,
but less gainly. Plucky,
the spider, I figured, said, *Okay:*
I'm 'Feeling Lucky'—*I'll* have *you, Compadre.*
Let's do it. The bug looked wrong—&
bumblingly deadly.
I plump for the spider, a black one.
The 'wasp' is just too Science-Fiction

Anyway, the woman gone—
I can't sing that song anymore.
('Directly'.)
And I can't watch till one of them
kills the other—I walk on.

Then, a moment later, I sang again.
Probably the same song.

SIXPACK TWO

Targa Florio

So we're racing around—it's the *Targa Florio*

or the *Mille Miglia*—Italy—& Phil has

the whole thing, notes on every *corner, hill, decline*—

on an endlessly long roll & he reads it out—"corner

at 100, at 115, change down—short straight, dip,

& brake for the next right" & so on. We're going

quickly, hours into the race. A bird swoops down

& into the windscreen & bounces off & in

the surprise—large black shape smashing against

the window—the roll goes missing. I'm coming

to this long, long turn, fast, that crests a

gradual rise then drops away.

You've got to be in fourth ideally & flying

but take your foot off the accelerator. This turn

every time will give you a different degree of instability

at just this point. You're now going down, just perceptibly.

There is a sudden view of the large plain before you.

Beautiful but distracting. And you see where you are—

in the middle, a bit to the side, or further over—the car

will wobble maybe, & you will catch it—then down

to third which slows you for the turn at the bottom, a

harder right—& accelerate again. I say to Phil,

Look, if you're going to shout Jesus Christ! at

every corner I won't be able to continue. Don't look.

Just put your head down & tell me … the um, the story

of your first marriage—everything you remember.

The boredom was so uninteresting I was able to

concentrate again, on the roads, the verges, the camber,

the engine sound, while he maundered on.

We lost it when a farm truck appeared ahead

across the road carrying a load of high-stacked grass.

Kabung! (lost a light & the front mudguard

& bent the steering.)

                        "Phil," I said, "stop now.

I don't want to hear it."

Bridget and Tanya, the Top Dog Grooming Salon, Richmond

Alice said a winter clipping, for Trixie,

the miniature poodle in cage number four.

If I owned a dog, it would have a dignified name—

Alistair or Dorothea.

Sometimes, but less now, I miss Rex, the kinesiologist.

Towards the end of our fling, he got high-handed,

suggested that I "accept" myself. I accepted his dandruff.

He never discovered my nickname for him—Snow Predicted.

Men—they've got a lot to learn about squeezing and pleasing,

most don't shower enough or in the right regions

and don't get me started on ear wax.

Still I'm not ready for celibacy,

might try sleeping with a woman.

Lila, who comes in every three months to sharpen our scissors,

well, one time, the way she looked at me, while I was clipping,

I nearly cut off a golden retriever's ear.

Leo Vetmeyer visited by journalist Roderick Bix

I paint what's there, who's there.

Objects *are* easier to depict than people.

A china egg cup, for example—

chipped on the rim, sits where positioned,

not complaining about the traffic, the government, a troublesome knee.

But portraiture intrigues. I work to pierce the defences of the sitter, which can

still be present when they are sprawled naked on the sofa.

In a voice quieter than theirs, I place opening questions about origins,

childhood interests, then pause for tea and a biscuit.

I use patience, flattery, sympathy where needed.

And the session and the painting progress or a truce is reached.

The diary's opened, a future date is circled

and I accompany the sitter down the stairs,

encourage use of the bannister,

remind them of that knee,

which they seem to have forgotten

for a couple of hours.

A Return

"Rietveld!" you say, & look up—(It's Waldo)—
"I was *wondering* when." "I was thinking about
paying you," he says. "But a gun was cheaper."
"Right. I don't think you should shoot me.
You'll get caught. You don't know how to
do this sort of thing."

"It's just a trigger," he says.
"You squeeze it." The gun goes off—he has
shot you, high on the thigh, a flesh wound,
& looks uncertain of what to do.
You tell him, "Waldo, hide the gun—I'll get rid of it—
& drive me to Emergency. I'll tell them
it was a drive-by shooting. You say
you stopped when you saw me."

You drive together to A&E, Rietveld at the wheel.
"It was an accident," he says. "Waldo. Don't tell them that,"
you warn him. "You saw me in the street." He clicks on
the wipers, drives sitting forward.

"Forget about the money," you say,
"I'm getting out of this."

The Middle Store, Coffee

Some of the females, younger females,
place baby-carriages between themselves
& my table. I don't think it's a protective measure—
they hardly seem aware of me. "Sir?" a youthful gesture
indicates a space for my response. I well know

what to do—I point at the 'crockery' (I believe
it's called that) on the table near me, occupied
by young, bulky males all in overalls. "I'll have
one of those, please." "And to eat?" "Smashed,"
I say, but can't remember the term. " … " "I'll

bring you the menu," says the youth, "—we're out of avocado.
There's eggs done different ways, & mushrooms."
And he goes.
He returns: "And there's toast & cereal." "One of those,"
I say again, & point at the young men's table—

who fall silent briefly
& look at me. "A flat white," says the youth
(a 'waiter') & turns. This is exhausting.
What to say—*Bloody hell? Jeepers?* There are
various expressions. The waiter returns, places the cup

before me.

Straightens. "What the heck?" I say.

"Something wrong, sir?" the youth enquires.

"Fine," I say—to alleviate his fears, "also dandy."

The three young men

fall silent once again, stand abruptly, look to each other

& leave the table. They go to a van, get in.

They are looking at me.

At this point I communicate with the mother ship.

"Beam me up. I don't think I can do this. Beam me up.

No, it's not my appearance. I will proceed to the lane

behind the building—you can retrieve me there."

Saul Spink, retired carpet salesman, Toorak, 1958

Self-improvement doesn't appeal
so I drink, swear when I spill red wine,
tell the cat to not look at me that way.

There were parents united in their disapproval.
Now they lie in separate coffins
beneath cold tombstones
which no flowers grace.

The crowd, the club, the crooners on the wireless
are not for me.
Smash another glass, another mirror,
spit into the fireplace.
It's winter in all my veins.

SIXPACK THREE

In the northwest corner of the state

One dirt road, a scar from the air.

A general store. Cash register lit by candles

when the power goes.

Those who stop do so

to ask for directions.

Some buy a chocolate bar

to get the taste of local dust

out of their mouth.

There's a cemetery,

tilted tombstones.

Irish surnames, the odd Italian.

People still kill for gold,

but do it elsewhere.

Jeez

I come out, pat my pockets for the fags—
the fags I no longer smoke—& there's that guy, waiting
I guess. "Right, mate?" I say. Already I'm thinking
I could go another coffee. (If it wouldn't make us late—
& we haven't even begun—I'd get us all take-aways.)

He looks at me strangely—I mean, no look at all—
miles away—as tho something is climbing up his pants
or he can hear jungle drums. I say, "Right, mate?"

& he's gone!

I tell the guys in the van. I'm pretty shaken,
to tell the truth. "Gone?" "Yeah. He just goes pale,
a bit transparent—then I see he's about
a foot off the ground, & half a sec later
he's not there." "Wow. Um, want to lie down for a bit?"
"No. But how can I stop thinking about it."

"The nut dressed in white?" "Yeah."

Vikal Irawan, Jakarta

The traffic is moving slowly, but there are

things to think about, & you think them, rolling

a cigarette. (He winds the window further down,

watching a motorcyclist's Hawaiian shirt lift

& settle slowly in the breeze—the hem of it—lift

& hold & fall, his engine revving & slowing

almost in time with it as he waits for the traffic to

move: the shirt is blue chiefly, but with white patches & small

motifs—

a dancing girl, a surfing man, palms, an

old plane. If it's the sort the Americans used,

a Catalina—if British, a Sunderland. He saw

the last of them as a kid, watched them arrive with his

father. Before them both were the Dutch. He has

an uncle in Rotterdam, from whom he has not heard

in some time, very old now. He left—& survived,

tho to live in that very cold land. They had been

each other's best friend, the brothers. His father & his

uncle. He remembers watching those planes

flying in to the harbour, hand in his father's hand.)

The traffic begins to move, no time for another cigarette.

Foot off the clutch, the car begins to roll forward slowly.

Brenda makes a new friend at
The Dapper Rabbit

Yeah, this frown isn't secondhand.

I've got worries. Dog worries.

Belair, my ancient Labrador has got these warts,

scratches at them until there's blood,

got some on her favourite plush toys.

She's overweight. My fault.

Got the equation "Food is love" from my mother.

I should go more often to her grave,

but she's buried out in Ringwood.

The *traffic* on the M1 these days.

Tell me about yourself,

but not too much.

I've got to go in 10 minutes.

They're screening *Thelma and Louise* at the Astor.

Before your time, probably.

I first saw it with my mother.

Now I'm getting teary-eyed.

You can buy me a drink if you like.

Shane, isn't it?

Arnold is glad it's Friday

A rough week at the supermarket.

A customer in aisle 7

tried to reach a bottle of olive oil on the top shelf.

The bottle tilted, started a chain reaction

and there were 5 one litre bottles smashed,

oil seeping into the chocolate aisle

where two boys, about 7 years old, maybe twins,

competed to see who could slide further.

Of course, Bennett, was out on the loading bay,

yelling into his mobile,

outraged over his wife's weekend spending spree

at Country Road and Uniqlo.

He'd seen the amounts on his banking app.

Bennett ended the call,

and, almost in tears, asked Vince,

"How many cashmere cardigans does one woman need?"

Vince didn't answer,

moved towards the rear of the storeroom

to check on a delivery—

two pallets of tinned tomatoes,

he'd ordered three.

The Courage Of Their Convictions

(Four Types on the Overland Train)

girl doing her eye makeup with great attention
to detail—quite deliberate gestures
repeated again & again. The mirror.
Finally, perfection. *The tired worker*
slumped, head back (like Courbet's
self-portrait—handsome, arrogant?
but he is sleeping, so 'handsome'). *Also*
'like art'—a young woman in blue
but tight overalls, great shoes, backpack—
slightly Spanish & '19th-century', like
a Manet—the piper, the soldiers
shooting Maximilian. *The worried*
'clerk'—pronounced a la American
"clerk"—gormlesss, nervous, suited.

But you get off before any of these.
What will become of them?

SIXPACK FOUR

'Dutch' Irawan

'Ivan' Irawan—formerly 'Dutch', & before that, back home,

 Joyo Irawan (sometimes called 'Comrade')—hands in his pockets,

was smoking a cigar.

The smoke blew away from him in a quick

blue-grey line, in a wind that was whipping down the coast.

He looked further right.

A long flat landmass across the water echoed the beach he stood on,

the water a grey that became warmer—in patches, and as it grew closer

to the far land. He had come to Vlieland, the West Frisian Islands

to see the sand dunes—& moving, sluicing water, wind & spume,

the subtle, and always unstable colouring, of sea, sand, mud & sky

so poetically described in *The Riddle of the Sands*. Holland overall

was flat—so none of this was unexpected.

It *was* beautiful—not even bleak as you became used to it.

He had come in spring. It would be too cold in winter.

The gulls & terns that flew, or were blown by

were the same as he saw on De Kreupel Island, or where he now lived,

near Velsen (in Kennemermeer, a small suburb near a peninsula.

There was even a connection to back home—it was the birthplace

of a seventeenth-century commander, Willem De Vlamingh, sent

to find a Dutch East Indies functionary, Admiral James Couper, who had ruled

much of Batavia, but been lost near the end of his career, 'at sea'

on a last voyage. Vlamingh had charted

some of Western Australia, given the Swan River its name—
& Rottnest ('Rat's Nest') Island. *The Riddle of the Sands*
had been hard, but pleasurable, to read:
the most beautiful language
for tides & winds & sands—*for the Zuider Zee*, which Ivan
had come to know since he'd retired from dock work and left
Rotterdam. Thirty years in Rotterdam. Become, almost, now,
a Dutchman. An 'Indo' perhaps, for some. For himself, *still,*
residually, *but definitely,* subtly an Indonesian. Indonesia
torn from him, like the scent of his cigar. He puffed again.
He will write to his brother's boy, Vikal. "I wonder how he is
doing?"

At Woolworths, The Hive Shopping Centre, Abbotsford

Arnold knows the drill.

Rotate the yoghurts, especially the lactose-free varieties.

Never let the level of the frozen chickens

in the central freezer cabinet drop to one layer only—

items which look like they're running out

make the customers panic.

They grab the last ones

and hey presto, you've run out.

Then you're behind the eight ball,

climbing over pallets

in the warehouse freezer room,

looking for size 6, 8 and 10 frozen chickens.

No more size 10.

You're on the phone to Steggles to order more

and of course, Brenda the assistant manager picks up.

She starts talking about her new retriever, Rojo,

who's got a cyst, on his belly, near where his testicles used to be.

You interrupt. "Brenda, I need 150 size 10 and I need them pronto.

Get 'em to me before the lunchtime rush and I'll buy you as many

margaritas as you can handle at The Dapper Rabbit on Friday."

Composed, Arnold straightens his name tag.

He can hear the manager paging him over the public address.

This doesn't faze Arnold. He'll start talking backlog, supply chains,

before Bennett opens his mouth, touch Bennett on the shoulder,

tell him how well the yoghurts are selling.

Nev Waldon, Steggles branch manager, talks to Brenda

Marj is on to me to get a dog
and pushing for a poodle.
I've agreed, but have certain parameters,
lines I won't cross—
so not a Standard poodle,
the bigger the dog, the bigger the poo, right?

Not a toy poodle either—too yappy
and with my size 13 feet
there'd be the temptation…

Marj and I have settled on a miniature.
Not white—the mud would show.
I reminded Marj of the shag pile carpets.

There's a black miniature on sale down in Tooradin,
the last one of a litter
and $500 cheaper than city prices.

She's already thinking names.
I'm going to have to be firm there.
I wish I could be so assertive
at our weekly sales meetings.

Doctor Harold Mathews on Holiday, Italy

The country air sweetened the bitterness in my mouth,
and feeling a little lightheaded, I walked on in growing ease.

A sudden excruciating pain in the lobe of my left ear
shattered my contentment. I shook my head,
thinking I had been stung; the pain increased.
Hearing a voice behind me, I turned to see a hawk-faced,
black-haired man of terrifying size
emerge from a nearby grove. He carried
a slender fishing rod from which a slack line,
dripping slightly, rose to the side of my head.

"Whoa there!" he cried reassuringly. "Well, I knew
the black gnat fly was a great fly,
but I didn't expect to catch anything *this* big."

Stopping near me, he continued: "Capeesh English?
You're American? I'm real sorry about the backcast,
but if it had to happen, it's just as well it was me
that did it. Don't you move & I'll repair the damage.
First let me introduce myself, Harry Mathews of Bellevue
Hospital. Keep still now, & I'll make it as painless as I can."

Taking from his lapel a large needle, which he charred
in the flame of a Zippo, he began manipulating my ear lobe.

"Say, that ear's infected." The hook came out with a
mild twinge. The doctor looked at my ear & whistled.

Drunkard at Potzdamer Platz

your inner Kirchner

your inner Beckmann

are good to call on here

(beer & cigarette,

 respectively)

your inner Kippenberger

(what drug are you *on?*)

You sway (slightly)

the sophisticated

Walter Brennan

runs interference.

Let's be clear, a voice says, in your head—

your voice, pretending to irony.

Is this another drug? or are
Kirchner & crew 'spirits'
just somehow available? (Mustn't fall into
the traffic)

Each yellowed page

How lucky to have been washed ashore,
cast upon this temperate island.

Initial days of fear.
Snakes. Bush pigs. Lightning.
Then the cave discovered.
Shelter. Unbroken sleep.
All bruising gone.

In numerous upturned shells
I collect rainwater.

After practice in the warm waters
of the shallower lagoon,
I'm now quick enough
to capture the more placid fish
with my bare hands.

Several moons ago, in the rainforest,
I found a book—
Nose Reconstruction—A Guide.
The illustrations captivate me, I intone
the words "Dorsum" and "Columella" out loud.

I no longer scan the sky for planes
or the sea for vessels,
even though the fever
sometimes returns,
rages through me.

SIXPACK FIVE

Timing

Summer's coming
and Shane's hinted at Hayman Island.

Brenda's never been
to a resort or Queensland.

She's yet to tell Shane
about her runaway years—
the brothel in Kalgoorlie,
the stolen motorbike,
the winter break-in—
her aunt's holiday house on Kangaroo Island,
to go cold turkey.

Questions. Inquiries. Prodding.
Interrogation rooms. Over-the-hill embittered cops,
who just want to hit you. Toss the paperwork.

Brenda looks at her wristwatch.
Shane's late.
He'll be apologetic.
Brenda's not used to that.

From Out Of The Past

"Rietveld," says the voice—a greeting.

I look up. I say, "How are you, it's been a while."

"Good." "How's the leg?" "Never notice it. All

good. How's," he says—& I can tell he's thinking, "'Paul',

is it?" "Stefan," I supply the name. "He will

be twenty now?" he guesses. "Nineteen," I say.

"Moved out—a girlfriend—University.

We miss him." "They all leave home. You'd want them to."

"The money…" I say. "Pimenton? Pimento? You

got some of those?" He holds up a small tin,

Spanish or Portuguese, glamorous young woman, & guy,

advertising the pleasure paprika can bring—a whole

life-style is indicated. "The money's cancelled, Waldo," he says,

"Forget about it." "Seriously?" I ask. He says,

"Cancelled. Different line of work now. I'll

get some cheese too—Romano & feta. The money

was never mine." He will catch my eye only fleetingly.

"I'm no longer that guy," he says, tight-mouthed.

"No longer a hard man? tough? bad? How've

you managed that?" I ask, "if you don't mind my asking?"

He

frowns, looking hard at the anchovies, caponata.
"Now I'm someone who *used* to be bad. I can
feel guilty about it, but it no longer controls
my life, my choices are all before me." He looks away.   "Roles
I didn't enjoy playing I don't have to play. Like a school

      bully who pulls his head in.

The person I thought I was—I'm beginning not to know him."
He pauses. "Waldo, you owe me nothing.
Give me some olives—kalamata."

Tight Focus

Yes, someone played a recording of that interview

not long ago. So I remember it all right,

& the occasion he talked about. It was

a distressing time. I was plunged, really, into a

recent past I had denied. I remember keeping

my head down, forced to look at just my

feet, the drive shaft, the stick—

which he was always wresting with. I recalled

the whole history … in representative fragments—passages—

when we first met, happiness, arguments,

my own selfishness—*& hers* perhaps. We were young.

He said 'Go on', a couple of times, or 'Continue', but I don't think

he was listening. I went on because suddenly there it

was—a history—slightly shaming, but actual—

the real thing, my life & character caught in one long

emblematic moment. We drove for an hour like that,

before we hit the truck. I was glad to stop.

Tho I couldn't stop thinking about it.

Yeah, no. We raced together a few more times. The last

time was in Bari. The crash in Sebring I took

as a warning.

Brenda's weekend unfolds

At a guess it's gone noon, maybe 1.30.
A dream last night—
I was a salmon swimming upstream,
resisted a lure.

That ringing. Probably not the telephone.
The band were *loud*.
Between sets I talked to the drummer,
flirted a little. He left with someone younger.

Oh well, I'll see Shane tonight at The Dapper Rabbit.
I hope he doesn't get that job in the Pilbara,
but Shane's restless.
I notice him stare at his car keys sometimes.

He doesn't know about me and W.A.
Which is how I mean to keep it.

A full tank

Shane driving out along the Western highway.
Then lesser roads,
kangaroos bounding
into the deeper dark.

Slow. Brake. Reverse.
Parking the car
flush against the railing
of a lookout point,
to smoke and think.

There were choices.
Perhaps Mildura, then Renmark
and on to Alice
or Portland, then Robe
and on to Adelaide.

Of course
Brenda would hate him for a while
until she found the envelope,
the three thousand in cash.

Maybe she could open
that hairdressing salon
she talked about
whenever she got plastered.

Shane started the car again,
decided on Robe.
He needed a bolthole,
to breathe in
some sea air.

A Visit to the Gallery

                         "Can it be? How very nice
to see you. It's been some time—we'd begun to
miss you. How *are* things?" "So-so." "Oh.
What brings you here?" "Antony, you're my dealer."
"True, & I'm glad of it, … but it's been a while."
"I'm not the sort who hangs about his gallery, insecure,
needing praise & reassurance." "No. You never were,"
says the gallerist. "You're welcome here—you know that—
any time." He looks at his artist. "In those first years
your advice steered me through some difficult moments,
towards good decisions that, on my own, I may not have
arrived at." "No doubt. But you'd *inherited* my contract—
the whole stable—why should I see you go down?"
"Quite," says Antony. "I saw," he continues, "last week
we sold *Lucifer I*—to Lewis. What's going on?" "Lewis has
left me." "*Lewis?* Why? I shouldn't pry. I'm sorry. It seems
unimaginable. How are you feeling?" "I hadn't seen it coming.
No doubt I should have," said the artist.
"Said he was bored." "Bored?" "He said, 'It's boring.'
Which seems even worse." "The office said you'd
rung thru, to arrange a lower price. In the circumstance
we'll take a lower cut. (Neither of us will make much on it.)
So," says Antony, "you're a little 'down'." "With everything—

the whole art thing, my painting, Lewis ... " He looked balefully

at a filing cabinet, "& I'm not selling."

"Are you painting? It's been group shows

for a year or two now. You've passed up the solo spots

we've offered." "What's the point? The critics just repeat

the word 'sombre' over & over & say that I'm 'respected'.

They review my reputation not my pictures." "Well

show them something." "Sombre, sombre, sombre.

Is he still, doc, you know, 'sombre'? do you think

he will 'pull thru'?" "You can have a show if you've

got the work for it. Are you painting?" "Yes.

I am actually." "*Lucifer* was a return to form."

"Lewis was leaving." "Ah." "But there are more."

"If you want to *sell* more your palette should be lighter."

"Ah." "But I don't expect you to take that advice. It's

not advice. Claude's prices, tho, reflect the truth of it." "Hartigan's

bubble will burst." "Maybe so."

SIXPACK SIX

A Visit to the Gallery II

"Hartigan's bubble will burst." "Maybe so,"
says the gallerist. "You found him for us—if you will
remember." There is a silence. "Yes. He's risen
up & up. He won't be able to sustain it. Still, he's one of ours.
He has another season at his current pricing.
If his prices drop, he'll move to leave. That is
the usual reaction." "Will you try to retain him?"
"Yes. Tho I'd let him go if he wanted." The gallerist
watched the other, "But I wouldn't push him."
They looked at each other. "Your work is highly regarded.
Make any new moves & they will be closely attended to.
If you want some *dates*," he said, "October could be yours.
Or the following … April-March?" "I'll think about it."
"October I'll hold for another month or so." "March."
"March? Good. This is exciting." The gallerist
leaned back in his chair. "So what's Lewis—
what's Lewis doing?" "He's on a trawler boat off
northern Queensland, I think. Although he may be
in the Pilbara." "Lewis? Extraordinary."
"He's pretty handy." "I had no idea."

In a Northern town, 1943

Miriam Fenner has never ventured abroad.

To imagine India is best,

besides she has a booking for one,

each Saturday night at The Raj,

Cottlebick's only Indian restaurant.

Mr Thorpe, also a long-term lodger

at Fernwood Guest House,

gets irate over any appreciation aired

for the foreign—food, books, motor cars or people

who he refers to as "hordes" and "droves".

Those familiar with Thorpe's outbursts at dinner,

resist provocation.

The salt is passed to widow Jenkins

who is trying her English best not to slurp her soup.

Mr Thorpe reminds all

of *his* favourite foods. Tripe. Kidneys. Liver. Tongue.

Mrs Barrett, a staunch vegetarian, dabs at her lips

with a napkin, excuses herself from the table.

"There's a discussion of Edith Sitwell's poetry on the BBC.

I dare not miss it."

Stella, the serving girl, arrives with her trolley,
removes bowls, plates, cutlery.

Mr Thorpe has a letter to write to *The Times.* A complaint,
probably. Rising prices, lowering standards…

The dining room empties.
Stella, in the kitchen, sighs, "It's like being in a novel."
She lights a Woodbine,
checks the packet. Five left.
She'll have to ration them until she gets paid. Friday.

Come rain or come shine

Miriam doesn't have any photos of Lieutenant Willis.
She knows that in recollection, events are embellished
but she believes their feelings were genuine.

The park bench, "their" park bench, which Miriam
passes on her daily walk, brings that May back into focus.

He, with American confidence,
led her on their first nocturnal stroll,
past The Star and Unicorn Hotel to the park.
After further talk of her birthplace, Liverpool,
and his, Omaha, he kissed her.
It wasn't brazen and he sensed to stop, that night,
when the evening had been as glorious as war allowed.

Bill, as he asked Miriam to call him,
couldn't let her read the telegram.
The next troop train to a place called Dover,
he'd heard of it in a song.
Miriam remembers sobbing in Bill's arms.

He never wrote.

Miriam believes he must have been part

of the D-Day invasion,

died on a Normandy beach.

At Fernwood Guest House

when there's a war movie

on the television in the lounge

Miriam goes out for a walk,

regardless of the weather.

A Revised Judgement

When she came to the turn-off that led to the cathedral,

she stopped & looked back down the sloping street,

& again gave the impression

of seeing all this for the first time—or of saying

farewell to it, after a long acquaintance.

Which is sometimes the same thing.

                              It was prettier

than she had seen it. A vast industrial street cleaner came—

almost like a sight-gag—to impugn this understanding,

& a gendarme arrived—to remonstrate with its driver—

& restore her recent judgement. She stepped down

off the rounded flagstone dais that supported the square's

central fountain, & stumbled, fell into the traffic

& was hit by a bus. The gendarme hurried to her,

but too late. The bus was neither ugly nor pretty,

it was just a bus. A little red mark showed,

near its light, where Helen's head hit it.

Are They Here Yet?

The Conversation Room, called that

because it is too small for large meetings

& has no TV, is where they meet—Thursdays, but sometimes

impromptu. There's Barry, he comes along. Popularly

regarded as a buffoon or an idiot, he is *very*

full of opinions—though he, almost literally,

never believes a thing anyone tells *him*. Which makes him

a 'known quantity' & hence, tho tiresome,

ineffective. He has persistence. Vera, despite her

name, is no friend of truth, as Margaret remarked.

Vera brings cake &, usually, sandwiches—&, if

anyone comes with wine, has usually collared it to bring

to the table herself—so that it appears part of her

gift. Her 'gift' is for *organisation itself.* Steven

comes, & Edwina & Jim. Jim sits here now, early,

doing a sudoku, a pie on the table by him

on the white bag that it has come in. No flies on Jim.

His face is flushed & he has a wide mane of hair a little

like Michael Heseltine's, if anyone remembers him—

somehow loud & clamorous, imposing, like a doubtful

press release. He does not believe in sudoku, rarely

finishes one, but they give him an air of 'getting things done'

& he is very can do—as a type, not as a point of fact.

He's 'doing' one now. "Jim!"

Lieutenant Willis writes to his brother, Walter Willis, 6 July 1944

I'd rather carry a squealing pig through three cornfields

than write a letter, but here I am, in a military hospital

in Rouen, northern France.

They pulled two bullets out of me.

Had one in the stomach and one in the neck.

I've got my appetite back

for breathing and eating unaided.

For a while, Camille was spoon-feeding me.

A nurse here.

She wheels me out to the balcony

when there's sun.

I'm working my way through

a dog-eared French-English dictionary,

learning the polite words first,

try some out on Camille each day.

You'll notice I've mentioned her twice already.

Confession time. Nurse Agnes, a sharp cookie,

has noticed how I turn my painful neck

to follow Camille's movements around the ward.

Nurses Agnes has become my language coach,

patient, but prone to giggling,

she's been teaching me French terms of endearment.

I've got to get the timing, the lightness of tone right,

before asking Camille, "How are you today, my little cabbage?"

Well, that's the state of play here. Write to me when you can.

Let me know what words you and Aunt Maggie

chose for Pop's gravestone.

I think of you all, safe in Nebraska.

SIXPACK SEVEN

The Alphanoia Psychology Centre, Ealing, London

Petra has finished vacuuming the Freud Room,
heads towards the Jung Room.
In the hallway she encounters a dozen elderly patients,
overnighters, still in their pyjamas.
Each clutches a teddy bear.
Petra, slightly hungover, remembers now,
Mondays here are "Childhood Recognition Day".

One patient, draped in a lurid pink dressing gown,
keeps banging the nose of her teddy
against a framed photo of Ludwig Wittgenstein.
Petra finds this disrespectful, but doesn't scold
"the poor dear", annoyed with herself for having
picked up this condescending English phrase.

"To be busy is good. That's my philosophy," Petra tells herself,
more or less, as she dusts the vases, wipes down
laminex surfaces,
scrubs at the inner rim of each toilet bowl.

Shannon Byrne, Actor

Byrne sits quietly & watches as members of the crew
come & go about him, carrying coffees & teas, sheafs of paper
under their arms, wiring, pieces of equipment. Some watch
episodes from the past—the show has never been screened
in this country apparently. Unsurprising. Some seem
to like it. This, the film version, being shot here
on the cheap, is intended to revive the fortunes
of the series, a boost to the audience that will guarantee
a long run of repeats. Which might work. The
series itself will end this year, word has it, & if not,
then the next. The sponsors have been pleased with it,
ratings haven't slumped. Down just a little.
Still, a natural end. Shannon had not expected
to become an actor—& then not a successful one—&
now it was over. He can hear the familiar theme music
coming from the monitor—on which he'll be appearing now,
wearing yellow hard hat, picking up his lunch pail or
putting it down—'up' if it's him going down the man-hole (the
beginning of the show), putting it down if he is
coming up (the show's end). Three people, backs to him,
are watching. One of them turns, reads his name
off his chair & addresses him, "Shannon Byrnes, is it?"
Shannon smiles encouragingly. "Ready, Shanno? You're on
in a moment. Been thru to make-up?" The guy
indicates the way to the set.

Where's Thursday?

Anna has come back to the tent to watch some more of
Where's Thursday?—which is amusing, & loveable, as,
she supposes, was intended, for being blandly retro.
The cheery theme is playing, & again the character Frank
Thursday is there, his head under a yellow safety helmet,
about to disappear down a manhole. Anna watches,
now, for maybe the fifth time. Shannon will smile,
give a thumbs up, grab his lunch box & disappear down
the hole. He is an electrical engineer. Down there he will
travel back in time to various eras & help with the wiring.
But more than that, he will become involved
in small domestic issues & crises & lend a hand,
often becoming good friends with the ancient Britons,
or Romans, or 18th century Londoners, Ming Dynasty Chinese
he has dropped in on. It is curiously reassuring that he
never goes forward in time. Down there he will sometimes
go past a big circular door labelled, ominously, 'TOMORROW'.
The camera will pause on it. But he never goes in.
So he'll be there back in the past, offering handy advice
on some young Roman daughter's betrothal, say, or her homework,
& fixing the wiring. People often remark
on how advanced Roman plumbing was. Apparently
the electricals were *way ahead of their time!*
Shannon's head will appear above ground at the end—
just as the foreman has yelled "Where's Thursday?!"
And that's how the episodes close. Sweetly funny.

Lost

Alberto's debut novel, *The Tide Masters,*
was now Hollywood property.

At the first script meeting, Myers pitched an idea—
"Hey, let's have a developer grease palms to have
his amusement park built on the beach."

Alberto countered, "That's not even in the novel.
The book is about the boy, Nathan, his relationship
with the beach and the dolphins."

"Look, I read your book. What you've got there
is too much thinking and zero *action.*
While you're typing on our payroll,
never forget that this is the *entertainment* industry."

Alberto swallowed.
Myers himself had driven Alberto out into the desert,
to all those illegal cockfights.
Alberto had borrowed money all over town.

There was sweat on Alberto's forehead.
He heard himself say,
"I've got this great idea for a beach buggy chase..."

A work in progress

Drawn curtains.

Joseph lies on the sofa,
thinking about his novel—
specific locales, the controlled revelation of each character,
the large tableau of two generations cast across three continents.
He's planned 52 chapters, one for each week of a pivotal year.

Carruthers of *The Times*, had described Joseph's last—
Wounded Days—as "compassionate but unwieldy".
He would head-butt the next critic who called his work "compassionate".
Then, there's Joseph's arch-rival, Pedersen,
bearded and prolific, who refers to Joseph's novels
as "doorstoppers".
Pedersen lives in a yurt on the Scottish island of Iona.

Joseph's years of forced labour,
winters survived in the gulag system
have left him distrustful of humankind,
sometimes of himself.

Anchored for now,

he accepts this current situation,

a flat without a clock or companion.

The publisher's deadline for *The Kolyma Saga*

has come and gone several times.

Small Boy On Holiday

one moment a baroque cupid happily capering,

minutes later, a lost figure, forlorn, tiny,

wondering at the cruelty of the world.

If he is having this ice-cream, now, at this

very minute, why isn't he happy? he wonders

& can't figure why or who to turn to.

The sustaining & enveloping attention

of the adults sometimes falters

& he is stranded, uncertain, bereft—

as people do the dishes, pack

items away, converse & joke & he is

suddenly unattended

for a vertiginous, or engulfing moment.

Then saved. A voice will say, "Harlan,

are you okay?"

SIXPACK EIGHT

Holiday—Peregian Beach, Queensland

Next morning—birthday breakfast for Yuki,

Harlan swims with his mum, dries off—& joins his grandfather

in defacing the noses of each face in the *Australian*,

the rule—one simple quick scribble. Job done. Incredulous

derision: for Querida-Inez someone, fashion-plate "life-style blogger"—

& another personality who, unwittingly, describes herself as

"plant-based". Gold Coast identities. The Noosa guy

who talked of "antidotal evidence", the fierce surf-warrior type—

tall, brown, tattooed & beer-gutted (& a 'noble visage'),

just stepped from a Reg Mombassa cartoon

—long grey curls, strong brow—sixty?

or not yet?—whom you had to admire.

Lordly, despotic, imposing.

An Aussie Ozymandias. Untroubled. Or

'cruelly', maybe, *'anticipating* coffee, juice'—

seen next door, from Hastings Street, number ten—

where you sat in the shade. From down south. Harlan

remembers—thinking—that the icecream & nuts &

chocolate that the surfy got looked nice.

Alan Chorva chats with Wayne Lech in the staff canteen, St Vincent's Hospital, Fitzroy

I get home,

flop on the couch,

Sonja hands me my gin and tonic

and she's straight into her *need*

to redecorate—from wine cellar to observatory,

and you know, my billiard table is out on the nature strip.

Sonja says it "detracts from the ambulance" or something.

It'll be me in an ambulance—heart attack from the invoices.

If I'm reincarnated I'd like to come back as a gas plumber.

They've already charged you a $150 call-out fee

before wiping their size twelve work boots on your welcome mat.

It was my mother who wanted me to be a radiologist.

I figure she must have seen a handsome one

on *Dr. Kildare* or *General Hospital.*

I do look good in a lab coat, especially if it's been pressed properly.

Hey, these doughnuts are good. New management.

Chocolate icing, and they haven't skimped on it.

I see you're trying the vanilla—that'll be me tomorrow.

Do you know anyone who'd like a billiard table?

The shack dweller

Anton's fleece-lined jacket hangs
from a rusted butcher's hook.

No books or paintings grace shelf or wall.
This is a scrubbed and swept realm
of knife, fork, spoon, dish, candle.

One day Anton will die.
Curious ants will crawl his body,
carry breadcrumbs
from his beard.

In the backyard garden
the shrieking wind will thieve
the scarecrow's faded hat.

Poetry Reading

Lex is listening, to a bloke who seems to be in charge,
who has intimated twice now that he will soon be off the stage.
Which is supposed to be a good thing.

It is easier to listen to than he had expected,
tho its not poetry, & it's not *that* easy either.

Janine's "varied ecriture" —(the guy quotes Peter Craven quoting,
with approval, 'Don Anderson' as saying)— *"masks a strenuous,*
almost pietistic, tightness of focus

on the problem of evil today."
*Craven himself goes on to say, "**That** this scrupulosity attains*
remarkable severity and sureness of judgment

is but the corollary of her work's moral heft
and the sheer muscle of its refinement."
Writing at the very height of his powers, Craven concludes …

and at this point Markou switches off. The Em-cee
goes on tho—*"Ethical to a fault, prim yet elegant—*
suave, soignée, truly stupefying".

"If I were Dean Martin," Dralex thinks to himself, "I would proclaim

'It's Amoré!'

or even **'Kiss Me, Stupid'**!"

"What are you doing here?" Sado Grescu slides in

beside him. "This isn't poetry," says Grescu.

"Can say that again," says another. "You'd know?" asks Markou,

"You write this sort of stuff?" "I do,"

affirms the stranger, "better tho." "Sado,"

says Sado Grescu introducing himself, "This

is Dralex," he points to Markou.

"Clive Zoty," says the stranger, who nods,

looks again to the stage.

Melbourne.

Alberto & Myers

My turn at the wheel & after twenty or thirty minutes

I pull the ancient Pontiac over, near a stand of tall

cactus plants and rocks, get out & go to the boot,

the dust from the car catching up, swirling about me,

call Myers—still counting his winnings—&, when he comes,

hand him the rifle. "Here, take this a second." He holds it

barrel up, pointing to the sky, I get out tools

in an old canvas sack, & a gun, & shoot him

with it. He looks surprised & I shoot him again, higher

up, in the chest, & he folds. (The movie's in the can now—

ruined, from my point of view, but sure to make money—

so I'm good for now. And it was a point of honour.)

I drag the body behind the three big boulders,

out of sight of the road. Exactly, pretty much, where I left

the man my wife said was Boz Scaggs or someone—no,

Billy Joel, tho I don't think it was him. The metal of the engine

is cooling down, making pinging sounds

as I return to the car, throw the gun in the boot & set off.

Back to Tinsel Town.

                    Different desert—

but those rocks looked just the same.

Same blue sky.

Dorinda Flett writes to her sister Abigail, 22 April 1972

I have been applying myself—
expect to get an excellent grade
for Home Economics.
My scones have been a hit.

There's a day girl, Beatrice. Bookish. Asthmatic.
She has a note from her family's physician,
is excused from Sports.
Beatrice writes poems.
In them glades, sprites, fog and shadows
are apparent or to be discovered
between the lines.
I've suggested that she brings them
onto *the main stage* of the poem.
I tried to present this as Beatrice's own idea
but she was affronted, went off to the library, sulking.

No, I haven't heard from Dad.
Both of us know the postal service from Rhodesia
is almost a fiction.

I will write to mother. Last time she traipsed around India…

I try not to dwell on that "incident". Our mother is our mother.

Hey keep me informed about Mollie Prescott, your new chum.

I'll dash now. Off to play tennis with an American girl.

I'll reveal more in the next letter

or—ha, ha—maybe I won't.

SIXPACK NINE

Wayne Lech talks to Wesley Brim, fellow intern at St Vincent's Hospital, Fitzroy

So I get away from the ward,
am seated in the canteen,
hunched over a burger, no onions,
when I get Theo pulling up a chair.

He wants advice, confesses
to friction, *issues* in his relationship with Tina.

Theo's clocked that me and Svetlana are back together,
appeared smoochy, glued to each other
at the staff Christmas party.

The truth is that Svetlana's still seeing Matteo, her personal trainer.
And by "seeing" I mean—naked, horizontal and thrusting.

I tell Theo to *listen* to Tina. There's too much interrupting
in the world, people elbowing each other out of the way.

Tina comes with baggage and none of it is Louis Vuitton.
She needs to spill, talk to Theo about her time as a street girl,
hopping into trawling cars.

He's green, though. Grass and spearmint green. His learning's all been
from books. Not from hurt, the low blues.

I'm an optimist, hope Theo and Tina get it together
in kindness and sex. A balance. Not out of kilter
like me and Svetlana.

Letter From Abroad

Dear Felipe,

      Greetings from down here—Coogee still—

& congratulations on the promotion. You say it

would have come my way, but I wouldn't have taken it,

I assure you. So you're my new boss. I remain older,

& taller, but there you go. I feel elderly-dolt

status coming on. Did McFerran leave the place

in good shape?

I'm extending my stay. I like Sydney,

& Helen loves it. My leg is getting better. By the way,

I was briefly under arrest down here,

a first time for me. Melbourne police had their

Sydney counterparts hold me, in connection

with some drug trafficking. Melbourne had wire-tapped

one of their (many, I gather) mafia gangs

asking incessantly when I'd be coming 'with the goods'.

Apparently they couldn't believe I wouldn't come

to Melbourne. The Sydney cops laughed. It seems

I was a mule. My code name—which I take exception to—

was Gold Fool. This was organised by Doctor

Veronika Stein. Remember her? I thought she was

a friend. She probably was, wearing different hats
or something. Compartmentalised. Some callipers she'd
given me—"just in case, Frank," she'd said—were filled
with Bitcoin codes & data. So, not drugs—theft. Anyway,
ha ha ha, right?

This is all the paper I brought down here. I'm on a bench,
in the park, near the big white pub. Bit of wind. The sea
to look at. The winters are mild here. Will right again.
Whoops—"will write again".

Frank

Impressions Of A Tourist—Re-visiting Brockley & Hackney, London

New Sainsbury's, new murals.
Cleaner, shinier, up market.
And Brown's, improved a little.

Voices of two stylish young women
talking—(friendly)—delicious vowels,
a casual friendship between them.
One is tall with wide shoulders,
narrow waist, a Picasso nose—
the 'Greek' sort, antic? antique?

The park at the top of the hill:
green & blossom. A man
doing tremendous sit-ups, radio
going quietly beside him
so much better than
gym music. He rests. Starts
again.

A small dog Cath catches
in her photograph sets off.

The green, the distant trees—you admire—
the women walking it (well ahead).

●

And—seven, eight years old?

The kid—Caribbean-British—in the park, behind his
talking parents—he strolls behind
yawns, clearly 'over it'. Going to school.
'Walking-him-to-school' certainly. Dad brief-cased
& suited, mother stylish.

The young girl: same age, coloured too,
with her mum. The girl in fabulous
clothing—'up for it'. Plaits, thin
black socked legs, on her back her
school bag

Helga Steckl, staff canteen manager, talks to
Troy Ulm, kitchenhand, St Vincent's Hospital, Fitzroy

How the younger male staff linger,

hunched in conversation,

worry lines creasing their foreheads,

often unnerved by the hiss of the coffee machine.

So *sensitive*.

Not my initial impression of males.

When our migrant ship docked in Perth,

forty years ago,

me and Magda took that job,

barmaids at The Kalgoorlie Hotel.

If I ever write a memoir of that time,

the title will be *Fools, Leers and Beers*,

my literary revenge

on the dusty place of my miscarriage...

Enough dredging.

Attack those saucepans, Troy.

Expect a rush on the lentil soup.

Grab yourself a fresh apron.

Henson will come snooping around

after the lunch rush.

I'll bribe him with a rice pudding,

sprinkle a little cinnamon on top.

He'll give us a tick on his clipboard

and be on his way.

Warehouse briefing

Your weapons are *to persuade*. To be used only
if Floyd gives the signal.
The driver's rehearsed the route,
is hip to traffic flow.

Anyone wounded, limping or fallen—
that's their solo experience.

In. Out. Away.
That's our trinity,
why this crew's the best.

Until Thursday
stay in your rooms.

Hand me your cell phones.
You'll be able to buy new ones
and a lot more
once there's no heat
and *I'll* let you know
when that's a reality.

That's all, gentlemen.

I hope to work
with all or some of you
again.

Light-Beams, Their Unbearable Weight

Anna Gerard rests during shooting …
She recalls for a moment her central role—as 'Ragged Blossom'—in the
John Bell-produced ballet, **Gum-Nut Babies**, based on the stories & illustrations
of May Gibbs.   She had toured later with the pantomime production
& a changing cast of celebrities—Emma Balfour, Vanessa O'Hanlon,
Paris Wells, even Tilda Swinton—as additional gum-nuts—Mick Molloy
as the lead 'Banksia Man', & Hamish Blake & Casey Briggs
as 'Bib & Bub'.

Popular but markedly different from her current movie—*LIGHT-BEAMS*
—a teen adventure set in rural Australia, in which a girl
builds an enormous particle *de*-celerator using
the midden of empties that generations of her
farming brothers & their ancestors have left
about the property. Anna's character employs the glass
to bend light, slowing it fractionally
at each 90 degree turn until, eventually,
having travelled hundreds of miles thru endless glass twists & turns,
it is deposited,
*as **matter,*** at the other end of the farm:
small bricks *of incredible weight & density.*

Somewhere else in the world

scientists become aware that the universe

is being subtly altered & the inevitable chase begins.

Lightbeams features the standard cast of Australian gothic weirdos:

Stork, Frank Thring, Noah Taylor, Nonie Hazlehurst as Anna's Mum,

& Peter Dutton—always shown with a pitchfork—

as the concerned fundamentalist farmer next door.

Mick Molloy as her alcoholic maths teacher.

SIXPACK TEN

Unlikely?

Anna Gerard, actor in the movie on the neighbouring set,

has left these for Shannon 'to look over' if he wants: synopses

her agent has proposed. Shannon looks at them, in a

cursory way. The Australian film industry.

Some of them seem to hail from the fifties—

some seem parodies, but to be half meant.

HARLOT BE WISE, a script of "extraordinary but touching

ineptitude" (says a Margaret Pommerantz), tells the tale

of the casual rise and rise of cheerfully feckless,

but readily opinionated, good-time-girl, Francine, who,

for free cigarettes, becomes a social worker — then advisor

to the Anglican Synod on social affairs—whom she embezzles—

before achieving an epiphany—and a kind of sainthood—

in the arms of her rather dim boyfriend—punk rock singer with

Danny Iscariot & the Lumpenproles—whom she converts—

Danny, that is, not the band—to Christian living.

And this—a 'religious boxing movie', REQUIEM FOR A HEAVYWEIGHT.

It features the canny but crooked Jewish manager of a jobbing boxer—

a drunken & bloated Russell Crowe. For a large sum Crowe

is to throw a fight but instead takes a major beating, collapses

& loses all feeling in his legs—& the manager … begins *to nurse him*
& to look after all the affairs of Crowe's dependent family
&, out of guilt, or duty, spends the rest of his life
supporting the large & emotionally needy household
of the crippled boxer—running their small, failing delicatessan business.
He becomes a kind of Christ figure, saintly, transformed,
a 'Christian' almost. A great little movie.

'Jeepers,' thinks Shannon.

The state of play

Derek's record label, Nothing Ventured,
has become *the one*.
Each morning the postman, Lawrence,
deposits numerous registered parcels containing demo tapes
on Erika's reception desk.
waits for her signature,
perhaps a smile.

Each night, often in the kitchen,
Lawrence tells Henry about his recent encounters with Erika—
brief descriptions of her looks and moods.

"Delicate silver camel earrings. Magenta lipstick.
Laughed at my elephant joke, Henry."

"A week since I detected her perfume.
At a guess Chanel No. 5,
a non-extravagant dab behind each earlobe, I suspect.
Her complexion—pale.
On the reception desk a 2B pencil,
snapped in half.
Conversation—polite, not elaborate—
the weather and Arsenal's chances."

"Well, Henry. Time for dinner.
First let me check
how your front left paw is healing."

Controlling the situation

Stan, the owner of the general store
is friendly but wonders about Shane.

Shane places a loaf of multigrain
on the counter to the right of the register,
answers Stan's initial questions,
decides to be pre-emptive.

"I'm on the lookout
for Asian paddle crabs, especially males.
The S.A. Government is concerned," he says.
"Nobody wants an outbreak,"
he looks at Stan. "The Limestone Coast
would become an aquatic boudoir,
though I've got to tell you
the conditions are ideal—
the warmth of the water, stable
saline ratio, the heat-retaining sand.
All reasons for *any* tourist to visit."

"I don't know about any crabs.
You'll have to ask my wife, Bettina,
a bit of a beachcomber.
She's in Renmark at the moment,
picking up a rescue dog. That'll make it four.
You wouldn't believe the price of worming tablets."

"Look Stanley, er—Stan. I can't stay and talk,
it's high tide. I have to secure further water samples,
then get them off to Adelaide."

Stan nods at this.

"This bread's good. I got the last loaf.
My lucky day," says Shane,

and walks out of the general store to the Land Rover.
The Glock 19 is there in the glove compartment
for sudden use
in case Stan or anyone
gets too nosy.

And These

Here on offer to Anna, Shannon sees,
is the principal role in *THE VERY NAUGHTY*,
a dramatization of the FBI files on certain women held
to be … 'of interest'—for allegedly threatening the state
in the 60s & 70s.

The treatment will exaggerate the already overheated imaginings
of the FBI & CIA, giving a lurid, comic-strip feel
to the subsequent movie—& making the lack of connection
& the *circumstantiality* of the case very funny:
Anna—who will be dressed very 'left-bank' throughout—
is always reading dangerously 'european' & leftist books,
looking at puzzling modern art, having affairs
with men unsuitably bookish, existential or of the wrong
race, or facial hair, or costuming—or given to playing bongo drums
or chess or smoking dope.

#

And this—a religious picture, set in Lourdes, where the heroine,
a very good—almost *'Christian'*— but, crucially,
atheistic young woman, employed to tend to pilgrims
… has a vision—just as her crippled charge—
a blind & bloated Russell Crowe—is miraculously cured.

Unfortunately, she *falls*, at precisely this moment,
hits her head & loses all feeling in her legs.

Crowe looks after her, taking her every day to the waters
to be cured.

She isn't cured, but he gradually falls in love with her
& becomes, himself, *a better person*.

Allegory & Isobel

Isobel looks at the pictures, looks at this one, reads

the wall panel beside, looks at the painting again—*Vices*

(Sloth, Envy, Tin-Ear, Cluelessness) *"calumniating"* (for that

is the word used) *Artistic Endeavour.*

'Endeavour' represented here, seemingly, by

Michael Douglas. (A look-alike.) The vices resemble

Gwyneth Paltrow, Edmund Gwenn, Gwen Stefani,

Scarlett Johansson. The male figure—Gwenn—would seem to be

'Drunkenness'—crown of vine leaves about the head, a

carelessly raised, spilling cup; the females are all

the less fun vices: envy, malice, etcetera. Their limbs long &

slackly muscled, pneumatic, nerveless, unconvincing.

'Ideas', she guesses. A tedious painting, apart from

its own silliness. It strikes Isobel that the most unedifying

paintings are precisely those that were regarded

in their own time as, above all, 'edifying'.

She thinks she might 'hate' allegory. Or is it

'neo-classicism'?

Clive in his Bellevue Street flat, Richmond, 1 July 2021

Clive coughed, spat into the wash basin.

Yes, a comma of blood there in the phlegm.

The years of smoking Gitanes had taken their toll.

Perhaps he had a decade left.

Time to finish his opus—

an extended suite of love and regret poems

about himself and Esther.

He was confident about the title—

The Mortar and Pestle of our Relationship.

Clive was pleased about the poems

set in Melbourne's ice-skating rinks

in Ringwood and St Kilda.

Esther in her sequinned costume

for the figure-eight competitions,

Clive consoling her when she lost.

Clive's 1972 speed skating trophy
was still there on the mantelpiece.
Clive saw himself back then— pitted against time,
focused on leaning into each curve,
head, arms and legs shaved
to minimise air resistance.
Then explosive applause,
his slow bow to those in the stands,
a kiss blown to Esther
who was proud of him ...

Clive had heard the rumours
about Esther these days—a rooming house in Redfern,
arthritic, alcoholic, flakes of yellowed paint
from the bedroom ceiling in her grey hair.

Clive circled his writing desk, sat down,
picked up his Parker 51 fountain pen.

Outside the afternoon became dusk
and still he wrote line after line.

He paused, capped the pen,
shuffled towards the toilet,
stood before it,
urinated as accurately as he could.

SIXPACK ELEVEN

Maya Manipur visited by journalist Roderick Bix

My ancestors were camel traders.
Negotiation runs in our family
and an ability to detect the deceitful.

My mother is my hero.
One evening, when she was 16,
she heard two aunties in the kitchen
working out advanced details—
an arranged marriage.

That night, while the household slept,
she made her way to the port,
stowed away on a ship
which sported a Union Jack.

To this day my mother won't reveal
how she survived her first weeks in Liverpool.

Three years she worked in Nottingham as a live-in domestic
for aspiring middle class British-Indian families.
My father was a delivery boy then for Mr Patel.
Jars of spicy chutney and pickles,
packages of roti bread,
sachets of saffron, cinnamon quills,

dried chilli flakes, cardamon pods, turmeric,
all carefully arranged in two panniers
attached to a Raleigh bicycle.
Bumping down cobblestone lanes
to knock on doors and wait for an underling or child
to press a few warm coins into his hands.

One afternoon
that underling was my mother.
She told my father to wait
and brought him a cup of hot chai
laced with condensed milk
and that's how they met.

Today is their 30th wedding anniversary.
I'll telephone my congratulations.
They're not quite sure what to make of me,
an unmarried TV presenter
but I assure them that I'm happy.
I know they still hope
that one day I'll deliver them a grandchild.

Dairy Farm

A movie about *making* a movie—
one Byrne assumes never really did happen—
the Hector Crawford production of *DAIRY*
OF A COUNTRY PRIEST. In it the Australian Film Commission,
very excited to be funding what it thinks to be
a daring Australian re-make of the old French classic,
takes the title to be a typical grant-application typing error.

Not so.

Crawford pockets the money & films *Dairy Of A Country Priest:*
wherein Sergio Holas is a recently arrived Catholic Padre, who decides
to convert to Anglicanism so that he can *stay priestly* & *at the*
same time **marry his housekeeper** (in the film played by an
Anita Ekberg look-alike): they buy a dairy farm & *purchase*
a rotolactor & they're set up.

References to the rotolactor within the film are always
heavy with double-entendre & the cause of much laughter,
& sniggering, amongst the audience. Canned laughter,
it goes without saying. *Dairy Of A Country Priest*,
say the notes, is slated to be continued as a TV series—
rather after the fashion of *Green Acres*. Was that a
good thing, Shannon wondered? Was it wishful thinking?

Checkmate

Shannon looked at the typescript, *THE ENEMY BELOW*—

a WWII submarine-versus-destroyer movie. A bearded, wily

U-Boat commander, steeped in humanist high culture, &

the same actor playing, *un*-bearded, the US destroyer Captain—

a little more homespun &, 'therefore', democratic—but again,

not a big speaker. The movie features—twice—

one of Shannon's favourite lines from movies of the era:

"The waiting is the hardest part". Heard as the sonar

goes pinging, & the men below *wait*, sweating & uncomfortable,

& *the men above* are equally silent, so as not to be heard—

& to hear. Audiences themselves will begin to feel

the waiting is the hardest part, Shannon thinks,

as both captains engage in a game of chess, their

respective moves sent from one to the other

by morse code—a technical impossibility, as someone has

pointed out in the script's margin.

The comment is answered—by the author, by

the director?—*What were they expected to use—pigeons?*

Shannon laughs.

\#

And here was the offer for Anna to appear

in the remake of an old boxing movie from the past—

Requiem For A Heavyweight—a movie about

corruption & exploitation in sport. In the movie

Anna Gerard plays the young female boxer controlled

by Mick Molloy as manipulative trainer-manager.

The movie, *BABETTE'S FIST,* seems set to follow the usual pattern

in which one or both are destroyed—but then becomes

an increasingly escapist romp and farce when both characters

make to outrun prosecution & investigation

by *lighting out for the territory* & together opening a bar

in Darwin, **The Master Of Margaritas.**

The happy end is so far from the movie's dark beginnings that,

at its conclusion, audiences will be 'rather relieved' by the

retreat into innocence though not sure if it is warranted.

Two follow-up movies on the same pattern are planned:

"With this narrative swerve," says the producer, "we have discovered

a new genre, perfect for the Australian reality." Towards the end

of *BABETTE'S FIST* Mick Molloy transforms into a large black cat,

perched on the bar, & Gerard's character

begins increasingly to resemble Pauline Hanson.

Career move

At first Shane saw the job as a cover

but now he'd grown to like, take pride

in every aspect—

loading the wheelbarrow,

balancing the heavy load along each plank,

getting the wet cement to the right consistency

then spreading it evenly, not excessively, with the trowel,

positioning each brick,

checking with the spirit level,

and after six solid weeks, solely with his eye.

He found himself whistling old show tunes,

"Get Me to the Church on Time",

"If I Were a Rich Man",

"I Feel Pretty".

The nightmares had disappeared,

the reliving of the "incident"

when he'd shot that bank guard—

grey-haired, retirement imminent.

Shane felt that with this hard, focused work,

he was serving a penance,

but laughingly, one which provided him

with a tan and impressive biceps.

Shane looked up at the sky.

It was certain to rain.

Time for a smoke.

He'd learned to roll his own.

Shane and the Limestone Coast

Each morning a 6 a.m. jog along the beach,
then 24 one-arm push-ups, a quick shower,
followed by a comb through his hair,
quite long now.

Rigour. Routine. Readiness.
Shane was still watchful
for "wrong-looking" cars or persons
appearing, descending, surrounding…

He'd thrown his mobile into a deep rockpool.
A relief. He *never* wanted to hear Trev's voice again,
offering an "easy" job.
In the evenings he read Westerns
borrowed from the library,
was working his way through
the available McMurtrys and Zane Greys.

The modern world,
much of it was still the Wild West—
greed and power plays,
preachers and snake oil salesmen everywhere.

Nobody's Fault But Mine

I pull into the motel car-park, go in & register.

I sign in under Myers' name. I'll dump the car

somewhere later, call my cousin, arrange an alibi—

say I got a lift with him, *'all the way'*—will that work?

Have to think it thru, where I've been seen, etcetera.

(Maybe where we bought the beer: *we had a 'falling out'*

& I called my cousin.) I'm thinking about

Maria, all those years ago—before I went back to school

& studied. (The first time I never did. I just played soccer.

A waste of time. I was happy though, & I think

of those times quite a lot. A kid. I was happy

with Maria, too. Tho mostly, from then, all I remember

is the work. Farming, then trucking. Then jail—where things

turned around.) That guy. I haven't thought of him in ages.

He looked very surprised.

I shot him in the foot first, so he couldn't run away.

Senor Joel? I asked. No, no! he cried. I took a deep breath

& sighed & looked regretful. I think he thought

he was saved—but I was playing around. I shot him

& trucked the body the next day, up towards the border,

& went on to deliver refrigerators, & refrigerator parts, to Texas.

Maria & I, we split soon after that. I regret losing the Pontiac,

but it'll have to go. I bought it off her father.

SIXPACK TWELVE

Therese Neil & Joyo ('Dutch') Irawan

Therese looks at the low horizon, that is both feathery

(soft, almost tangible), & distant. Tho Joe informs her that it is close.

A matter of weather—air thick with moisture, fog, rain,

the skeins of different densities & temperatures: blues, plain

white, & a range of greys, entwined. A sky, of the same grey,

rose—'towered'—but looked down, she thought, with benignity.

A word no-one, any more, uses. No journalist—

unless to cover the Vatican. Therese's free-lance

work is winding down—her networks ageing, her scant

contacts fewer—retired, scattered, promoted. This

was an outcome she had foreseen—almost

upon moving here—an outcome to be staved off, resisted,

delayed but not avoided. She had made a good run,

extended her career in ways she'd not have done

had she stayed in London. She had listed

to herself, often, the reasons she preferred to be

English here, rather than English in England: definition—

one preserved a certain distinction in otherness, saw things

clearly, & abstractly, as an outsider—&, appearing

as different to those around you, your thinking, your opinion,

you yourself, were never entirely regarded as a known quantity.

      So, 'mystique'.

(No, not that, but something.) In England, by now, her life

      would have devolved to gardening—

"As it was quite likely to do in Holland," she thought happily,

but at least she had had those years, with Joe, of intensely

sharp thinking, of writing, & publication—reputation in a

      small way. Remaining,

in exile, as Brexit loomed … What to do about it? Joyo's exile

would never end, for political reasons—maybe unnecessary, but why

would you go back, test it? Twenty or so years now, a European, a Europe-watcher.

England? Would it suit him? England was an ideal he knew better than to test. Not the

climate, or the culture… In any case, Holland was a link with Indonesia. While

113

return was ruled out, the connection made him part of history

not an accident, not quite so displaced—part of the story.

He was the only one she knew who still read Conrad, Kipling,

Tennyson of all people, Austen, 'The Vanity of Human Wishes',

Arnold Bennett, Shelley, & enjoyed—both maliciously and yet sympathetically—

The Thirty-Nine Steps, The History of Mr Polly—alongside, say, Fanon.

His English, he had told her, had an American accent when he was young:

gone now, tho perhaps it slowed, made more dignified, his correct and slightly

old-fashioned manner. Joyo's perceptions were Marxist—& tellingly.

He could sound like a cultured leftist professor—one dressed as a merchant seaman.

He came in now, placed his cigar on the table's edge, took his cap off, shook

the moisture from his hair. He smiled at her—"Thinking?"—& watched her face

with pleasure. The week spent here, tho not planned that way, seemed

to both of them a significant break. What would they return to? He

smiled. "Nice out there," he said, "but we should get back? You can place

whatever you've been writing." "I've been thinking," Therese said,

"We should *decide* ..." "And?"—he looked at her, smiling. "I'd rather be

foreign, here, with you." "I'm a Dutch citizen," he said, & laughed—"& so

are you." "Dual citizenship," Therese confirmed. "But this way, Joe,

we're equal—both here from elsewhere." "Like spies," Joyo said.

114

"Do you think I'm like Burton, a little, in *The Spy Who Came In*
From The Cold? You look like Claire Bloom." She laughed,
"Well that clinches it. Were they happy, in it?" "It was sad—tho I forget.
But that was the movies. Books are the thing. It was cold out *there,*" he said,
moved to the stove, put the kettle on. Therese put her arm over his shoulder.

In the wee small hours

Clive didn't attend Esther's funeral
but paid for the hearse hire, the coffin, the flowers.
He had negotiated all of that by telephone
with Metcalf, the funeral director.

A telephone was the only modern appliance Clive owned.
Others told him—fellow poets— that he *needed* a computer
and an email address, but Clive refrained.

Clive liked the look of his fountain pen nib,
the slight scratchy sound it made
when he wrote with an anxious fury
across a notepad or the back of an envelope,
not wanting to lose momentum,
an inspired thought, a flurry of images.

Clive felt a stabbing pain,
clutched at his chest,
fell to the floor
in the book-lined study.
His ginger-haired cat,
sprung from the cushioned sofa,
licked Clive's inert face.

Clive looked into the cat's green eyes
some moments later. "Hullo, Puss."
"Getting to know you. Getting to know
all about you," Clive sang to it quietly.
The cat purred, blinked a few times.

Clive rose, called a taxi, fed the cat.
"Time for a little trip to A & E," he told it,
picked up a book to take with him—
recommended by Sado Grescu.
Gold Fools.
"Very inquisitive,"
Grescu had told him.

Brenda talks to Agnesa, the Ramkrishna Vedanta Ashram, Darjeeling, 5 May 2019

I miss home, Melbourne, Australia,
but less each day—
all the hustling and putting on a front.

The first fortnight here I found hard.
Sitting cross-legged, starting so *early*
and learning the prescribed breathing method.

I've shed weight and what you'd call *armour*.
It's helped that I'm away from family and peers,
some, who I can now see
strike out—and wound me and others.
In time, I'll be able to forgive them.

So tell me about your village in Albania,
how you made your way to India.
You seem humble and contained.

Driving through Fitzroy: with passengers
Antony Pierce, & Lewis Manne

The artist drove, Lewis in the passenger seat
& the gallerist behind. "So, Lewis,"
said the latter—"you're back." "He is," said the artist
happily, laughter on his face. "I saw the reviews,"
said Lewis, "knew he'd be in a good mood." "Is that
why you left, *moods?*" "Ha!" says the artist. "He needed
a kick in the arse," Lewis adds. Lewis wore a white, Mexican guayabera shirt,
straightened the cuffs—watched the nervous traffic
pause, as the Merc swooped down, into the intersection,
bounced & sounded the horn—imperious or careless,
but gaining right of way. Lewis spoke—& the gallerist
was surprised, accustomed to his silence—"We get along, always.

He wasn't doing any work. Nothing new."
Once more, the silence. "And wasn't about to." "I see."
"But I *have*. I *did*. So it succeeded, Antony," the artist
looked at the gallerist in the mirror—"Great reviews!"
"Yes," said Antony, "they position you
as a player again, & major." "'Dangerous',"
said the artist, "'malevolent', 'gravely sardonic'—that's my favourite."
Antony remembered talk of the Pilbara, Queensland trawlers.
"So what did you do?" he asked Lewis, to find out which.

"I wrote an opera."

New, hardly worn, surely sold
for one tenth the price. Finally.

The new jacket looks good

looks better & better the more Cath

wears it. Hangs just right

At last, thinks the jacket—*Someone who*
understands me. Finally.
Together we can do this.

That is what Cath thinks.

She enters the street boldly—

there's her bus. She swings on. 'Home',

in time to go out again

or to confirm her purchase in the mirror,

save it.

Clive and Claude are able to lunch today

Harry, the proprietor, no longer hands them menus.

Clive always has the vegetarian platter.

Calamari, chips and Greek salad for Claude.

Neither speak of their ailments. They are borne,

as are reviews and labels given

regarding Clive's poetry, Claude's paintings—

Minimalist. Abstract. Panoramic, Surreal. Jocular.

Both jazz buffs, Clive and Claude are interested

in propulsion, tone, atmosphere,

but beyond those enchantments—

gamble and break-through.

Certain parties in Sydney, London, New York City,

Athens and Barcelona are recalled.

Both agree it was Tara who nearly fell

from the balcony... Was she pushed?

There's a good-humoured tussle for the bill,

but Claude pays. Recently, an exhibition in Wellington.

Numerous paintings sold.

They leave Tsindos,

as Waldo Rietveld enters,

walk together down Lonsdale

not arm-in-arm,

but to hurrying passersby

it seems that way.

Notes

'Doctor Harold Mathews on holiday, Italy' is lifted, entirely, from Harry Mathews' novel *Tlooth*.

'A Revised Judgement' begins with lines taken from *The Evening of the Holiday* by Shirley Hazzard.

'Are They Here Yet?' attempts to borrow the manner of Richard Osman's *The Thursday Murder Club*.

It will be apparent to the reader that many of the film scripts Shannon Byrne reads—all supposedly from Anna Gerard's agent—are the product of one single script team: the preoccupation with falling, with being crippled, with redemption & so on. At least one film idea, though, derives from the memory of books by Bernard Malamud—*The Assistant* or *The Magic Barrel*.